Saving your Marriage or Relationship. A woman's guide

Evelyn R. Beacham

Saving your Marriage or Relationship. A woman's guide

Copyright Arthur Crandon 2024

All rights reserved. No part of this book may be reproduced, stored in a retrieval system, or transmitted in any form or by any means—electronic, mechanical, photocopying, recording, or otherwise—without the prior written permission of the publisher, except for brief quotations in critical reviews or articles.

This is a work of fiction. Names, characters, places, and incidents are either the product of the author's imagination or used fictitiously. Any resemblance to actual persons, living or dead, events, or locales is entirely coincidental.

ISBN: 9798343073706

Cover design by Lynnie Ceniza
Interior design and formatting by Lynnie Ceniza
Published by Arthur Crandon Publishing
Visit our website: Arthurcrandon.co.uk

DISCLAIMER

The information provided in this book is for general informational purposes only. It does not constitute legal, financial, or professional advice. While every effort has been made to ensure accuracy, the author and publisher assume no responsibility for errors or omissions. Readers should consult with appropriate professionals for specific advice tailored to their individual circumstances.

First Edition: August 2024

"Saving your marriage or relationship" is a practical guide for couples seeking to rebuild and strengthen their bond. Whether you're facing communication breakdowns, emotional distance, or unresolved conflicts, this book offers proven strategies to rekindle love and trust. Through clear advice on conflict resolution, rebuilding intimacy, and fostering healthy communication, it helps partners reconnect and restore harmony. Learn how to manage challenges together, grow individually, and create lasting happiness. Packed with actionable tips and real-life examples, this book empowers couples to navigate relationship difficulties and build a deeper, more fulfilling connection.

CONTENTS

	Acknowledgments	i
1	Assessment	1
2	Communications	11
3	Trust and Reevaluation	21
4	Intimacy	39
5	Emotional and Mental Health	57
6	Emotional Support	67
7	Work on Yourself	75
8	Re-establish Goals	85
9	Managing Conflict	98
10	Boundaries	103

Struggling to save your relationship? In this book we provide the tools and insights you need to turn things around. With guidance on overcoming common relationship hurdles—such as trust issues, lack of intimacy, and poor communication—it offers step-by-step advice to reignite the passion and restore trust. The book emphasizes emotional connection, respect, and patience, helping couples rediscover what brought them together in the first place. Whether you're on the brink of a breakup or just want to improve your partnership, this book will inspire and guide you toward a healthier, more loving relationship.

1 ASSESSMENT

Assess the Situation Honestly

Before attempting to fix a failing relationship or marriage, it's critical to take a step back and objectively assess the state of the relationship. This is often the hardest but most necessary step because it requires you to look at the situation with clear eyes and be brutally honest with yourself. Here's how to approach this:

A. Identify the Root Causes

Start by identifying the specific problems that are straining the relationship. This is more than just noticing the symptoms of a troubled relationship (e.g., constant arguments, lack of affection); it's about understanding the deeper, underlying causes of those issues. Common root causes include:

- **Lack of Communication**: If meaningful communication has broken down, misunderstandings, resentment, and distance can easily build. Are conversations with your partner more transactional than intimate? Do you avoid talking about deeper issues because it leads to fights or discomfort? This lack of open, honest dialogue often erodes trust and emotional connection.

- **Emotional Distance**: Have you noticed that you and your partner no longer feel emotionally connected? This might look like a lack of affection, empathy, or interest in each other's feelings and experiences. When emotional distance sets in, couples often feel like they're drifting apart.

- **Financial Stress**: Money problems are a major source of tension in many relationships. Financial disagreements can create an atmosphere of blame, guilt, and frustration. Are financial hardships causing stress? Are you and your partner struggling with different spending habits or financial goals? This can lead to power struggles or feelings of inadequacy.

- **Infidelity or Betrayal**: If infidelity or another form of betrayal has occurred, trust will be severely damaged. Has there been cheating or deceit? If so, the process of rebuilding trust is slow and challenging, and both partners must be willing to put in the work to heal.

- **Lack of Intimacy**: A relationship without physical or emotional intimacy can feel cold and disconnected. Are you experiencing a decline in physical affection or sexual activity? Has emotional closeness faded? Intimacy is a vital part of a healthy relationship, and a lack of it can lead to frustration, loneliness, and dissatisfaction.

- **Constant Conflict or Resentment**: Are you and your partner constantly arguing, even about small things? Is there a sense of resentment or bitterness that colors most interactions? This pattern of conflict can create a toxic environment and make it difficult to see the positive aspects of the relationship.

- **Differing Life Goals**: If you and your partner have grown apart in terms of what you want out of life (e.g., career paths, family planning, lifestyle), it can lead to feelings of frustration or disappointment. Are you moving in different directions, and is it possible to realign your goals?

Identifying the root cause of your relationship problems requires deep reflection. Write down or mentally note the main issues and be specific. This step helps you avoid blaming the other person for everything, giving you a clearer understanding of where things went wrong.

B. Take Responsibility

Self-awareness is crucial in any relationship. It's important to recognize that relationship problems are rarely one-sided. While it's easy to focus on your partner's mistakes or behaviors, taking responsibility for your role in the issues is key to creating meaningful change.

Ask yourself:

- **How have my actions or behaviors contributed to the current state of the relationship?** Did you neglect communication, or did you react with anger or defensiveness? Were you unavailable emotionally or physically?

- **What patterns do I repeat that might be causing strain?** Reflect on whether there are consistent behaviors or attitudes that you bring into the relationship that cause tension—things like criticism, controlling behavior, emotional withdrawal, or avoidance of conflict.

- **Am I fulfilling my partner's needs?** Relationships require effort from both sides. Are you actively showing love, support, and understanding? Do you neglect their emotional needs? It's essential to consider whether you've fallen short in areas such as affection, communication, or attention.

Taking responsibility doesn't mean blaming yourself for everything, but it involves acknowledging that your own actions or inactions play a part in the dynamic. Self-reflection and accountability are key to any healing process.

C. Evaluate the Relationship's Value

After identifying the root causes and recognizing your role in the problems, the next step is to evaluate whether the relationship is worth saving. This requires a deep, honest look at whether both partners still value the relationship enough to put in the effort it will take to fix it.

Ask yourself:

1. **Do we still love each other?**

    o Love is the foundation of any long-term relationship. Do you still feel a deep sense of care, affection, and connection to your partner? Is there an emotional bond left that can be reignited? It's important to differentiate between being emotionally invested in a person and being attached out of habit, comfort, or fear of change.
2. **Do we share the same core values and goals?**
    o If your goals and values have

diverged, is it possible to realign them? Are you still working toward common dreams and supporting each other's growth? Healthy relationships thrive when partners are aligned in their long-term vision, such as raising a family, financial planning, or career ambitions.
3.
4. **Is there mutual respect?**
    o Respect is non-negotiable. Do you respect your partner as a person, and do they respect you? Without mutual respect, it's difficult to maintain a positive, equal partnership. Evaluate whether your partner's behavior is supportive or if it undermines your confidence or self-worth.

5. **Are we both willing to work on the relationship?**
    o A relationship can't survive on the efforts of one person alone. Are both you and your partner willing to put in the work to repair the relationship? If your partner is disengaged or unwilling to change, you must evaluate whether it's possible to move forward without equal effort from both sides.

6. **Am I staying for the right reasons?**
    o Are you staying in the relationship because of genuine love and hope

for improvement, or are you staying out of fear, comfort, or pressure? If you find yourself staying for reasons like financial dependence, fear of being alone, or for the sake of children, you must weigh the long-term impact of continuing in an unhappy or unhealthy relationship.

7. **Can I envision a positive future together?**
   o Ask yourself whether you can realistically imagine a future where the issues have been resolved, and the relationship is fulfilling again. If you can picture both of you being happy, communicating well, and sharing love and support, the relationship might be worth saving.

Final Thoughts on Assessing the Situation Honestly

This stage is about gathering as much clarity as possible before deciding on the next steps. It involves taking stock of your feelings, your partner's behavior, and the overall health of the relationship. You need to face the hard truths about what's working and what isn't, rather than focusing on an idealized version of the past or future.

If, after honest reflection, you still believe in the relationship's potential and both partners are willing to work on it, then you can move forward with the process of saving and rebuilding it. However, if the core issues seem too insurmountable or if there's no mutual effort to improve, it might be time to reconsider the future of the relationship.

This assessment forms the foundation for moving forward—whether toward healing or a potential parting of ways.

2 Communication

Open, Honest, and Non-Defensive Communication: The Cornerstone of a Healthy Relationship

Communication is the foundation of any strong, healthy relationship. When communication breaks down, misunderstandings, resentment, and emotional distance can grow. To rebuild or strengthen your relationship, it's crucial to cultivate open, honest, and non-defensive communication. This kind of communication involves not only speaking your truth but also listening to and understanding your partner's perspective in a supportive and non-judgmental way.

Here's how to practice effective communication in detail:

1. Set Aside Time for Meaningful Conversations

In our busy, modern lives, it's easy for couples to get caught up in day-to-day tasks, often neglecting deep, meaningful conversations. Without these intentional discussions, partners can drift apart emotionally. Setting aside dedicated time to communicate without distractions is vital.

- **Create a safe space for discussion:** Choose a quiet, neutral environment where you both feel comfortable and relaxed. This might be during a walk, at the dinner table, or during a quiet evening at home—anywhere that allows you both to focus on each other without external interruptions (e.g., phones, work, or kids).

- **Make it a regular habit:** Scheduling regular "relationship check-ins" fosters a culture of communication. This could be weekly or bi-weekly, depending on your needs, but consistency is key. During these conversations, both partners should have the opportunity to express their feelings, concerns, or desires in a calm and respectful way.

- **Set boundaries for the conversation**: Agree on the time and space beforehand, and make sure it's clear that the conversation is about improving the relationship, not attacking each other. It's also helpful to agree on ground rules, like no interruptions or personal attacks, so the conversation can remain constructive.

This time should not just be about resolving conflicts; it can also be used to express appreciation, talk about future plans, or simply connect emotionally. Regular communication prevents small issues from snowballing into major problems.

---

2. Use "I" Statements

When discussing difficult topics, it's essential to focus on how you feel without blaming your partner. Using "I" statements helps to express your emotions without making the other person feel attacked, which reduces defensiveness and leads to more productive conversations.

- **Why "I" statements matter:** Instead of saying, "You never listen to me!" which puts the focus on blaming your partner, say, "I feel ignored when I try to share my thoughts, and I would really appreciate more attention when I talk." This shift in language focuses on your feelings rather than accusing the other person of wrongdoing.

- **Structure of an "I" statement: The general formula is:**
    - I feel + [emotion] + when + [specific behavior or situation] + because + [impact it has on you].
    - Example: "I feel frustrated when we don't discuss our plans in advance because it makes me feel like my opinions aren't valued."

- **Avoid absolutes like "always" and "never":** These words tend to exaggerate the problem and escalate the conflict. For instance, "You never help with the kids" can make your partner defensive, whereas "I feel overwhelmed when I handle the kids alone, and I'd love more support" opens the door for understanding and change.

Using "I" statements helps keep the conversation constructive, as it's centered around how you're feeling rather than accusing your partner, which can easily trigger defensiveness.

---

3. Listen Actively

Listening actively is just as important as speaking openly in a relationship. Often, people listen with the intent to respond rather than truly understanding what their partner is saying. Active listening involves fully concentrating on what the other person is communicating, both verbally and non-verbally, without preparing your rebuttal in your head.

- **Focus on understanding, not reacting:** When your partner is speaking, avoid interrupting or mentally planning your response. Instead, focus on truly understanding their feelings and perspectives. Listening attentively shows respect and a willingness to understand their emotions and concerns.

- **Validate their emotions**: Even if you disagree with your partner's point of view, it's important to validate their feelings. You can say, "I understand why you're feeling upset," or "That must have been really difficult for you." This doesn't mean you have to agree with everything they say, but validation shows empathy and reassures your partner that their feelings are legitimate.

- **Paraphrase or reflect back what you heard:** After your partner has expressed their thoughts, paraphrasing or summarizing their words shows that you were listening and provides clarity. For example, "So what I'm hearing is that you feel unappreciated when I don't acknowledge your efforts at home." This can clear up misunderstandings and gives your partner a chance to confirm if you've understood correctly.

- **Ask open-ended questions:** Encourage your partner to share more by asking open-ended questions. Instead of "Did that make you mad?" which leads to a yes/no response, ask "How did that situation make you feel?" This opens the door for a deeper discussion and helps both partners feel heard.

Listening is a powerful tool for deepening emotional intimacy and trust. It allows your partner to feel safe expressing their vulnerabilities, which is essential for a healthy relationship.

---

4. Avoid Emotional Outbursts or Defensiveness
5.
Emotions can run high during difficult conversations, but staying calm and measured is crucial to maintaining productive communication. Emotional outbursts—such as yelling, crying, or making hurtful remarks—often escalate conflict and cause long-term damage. Likewise, defensiveness (feeling attacked and responding by denying responsibility or shifting blame) can block any potential for resolution.

- **Stay calm and grounded:** If you feel yourself becoming overwhelmed, it's okay to take a break. Pause the conversation and suggest taking a few moments to cool down. For example, "I'm feeling too emotional to continue right now. Can we take a break and talk again in 20 minutes?" Stepping away allows both of you to process your emotions without saying something you'll regret.

- **Avoid "kitchen-sinking":** This is when, during an argument, you bring up multiple unrelated issues from the past ("throwing everything but the kitchen sink" into the conversation). This tactic overwhelms the discussion and often derails the main point. Stick to one issue at a time and work on resolving it before moving on to anything else.

- **Acknowledge defensiveness:**

- Defensiveness is a natural response when we feel attacked, but it can shut down effective communication. If you catch yourself becoming defensive (e.g., denying or deflecting blame), try to recognize it in the moment. You might say, "I realize I'm getting defensive. Let me take a moment to hear what you're really saying." This self-awareness allows the conversation to continue constructively.

- **Respond rather than react:** Reacting emotionally often leads to regrettable actions or words. Responding, however, involves thinking about the best course of action. If your partner says something hurtful, instead of reacting angrily, pause and calmly express how it made you feel. For example, "That comment hurt my feelings. Can we talk about why you said that?"

- **Use calming techniques:** If you find it difficult to stay calm during heated conversations, try deep breathing exercises or counting to ten before responding. This can help reduce emotional intensity and allow you to respond thoughtfully rather than impulsively.

By staying calm and avoiding defensiveness, you create a safe space for constructive dialogue. It also helps prevent discussions from turning into full-blown arguments, allowing both partners to feel heard and respected.

Conclusion

Open, honest, and non-defensive communication requires ongoing effort, but it is the key to maintaining emotional closeness and resolving conflicts in a relationship. By setting aside time for meaningful conversations, using "I" statements, listening actively, and avoiding emotional outbursts, both partners can engage in healthier and more productive communication.

Strong communication helps to rebuild trust, foster deeper intimacy, and ensures that both partners feel respected and valued. Ultimately, improving communication lays the foundation for resolving deeper issues in the relationship and cultivating long-term emotional satisfaction.

3 TRUST AND REEVALUATON

Rebuild Trust in a Relationship

Trust is the cornerstone of any strong relationship, and once it's damaged, rebuilding it can be a long and difficult journey. Trust can be compromised in various ways, such as dishonesty, neglect, emotional withdrawal, or infidelity. Whether intentional or not, breaches of trust create emotional wounds that require time, patience, and effort to heal.

Restoring trust is essential for a relationship to recover and thrive, but it cannot happen overnight. It requires both partners to be fully committed to the process, showing vulnerability, transparency, and a willingness to rebuild the emotional bond that has been fractured.

---

1. Be Transparent

Transparency is a key component of rebuilding trust, especially if dishonesty, secrets, or infidelity have played a role in the breakdown of the relationship. When trust is broken, the injured partner often feels unsure of what's real and what's not, leading to suspicion and insecurity. Being fully transparent helps to restore a sense of safety and security.

- **Commit to complete honesty**: If there have been lies or withheld information in the past, commit to being completely open and honest going forward. This means sharing details about your daily activities, your whereabouts, and any interactions with people that may cause concern to your partner. For example, if trust was broken due to infidelity, it's important to be upfront about who you're spending time with and where you're going.

- **Open up emotionally**: Trust isn't just about physical transparency (where you are, who you're with), but also emotional openness. Share your thoughts, feelings, and fears with your partner to foster a deeper connection. When one partner feels emotionally shut out, it can lead to further distrust. Emotional transparency allows your partner to see that you're making an effort to be vulnerable and real with them.

- **Avoid secrecy, even about small things**: If your partner feels that you're hiding something, even if it's small or insignificant, it can reignite feelings of distrust. For example, not sharing something as simple as a change in plans can cause doubt in your partner's mind. The goal is to create a space where your partner feels they know what's going on in your life, so they don't have to wonder or worry.

- **Be proactive in communication**: Instead of waiting for your partner to ask, offer up information voluntarily. If they've had concerns about a specific area in the past (e.g., spending time with certain people), make an effort to proactively inform them about any relevant details. This doesn't mean you need to check in constantly, but offering transparency without being prompted demonstrates commitment to rebuilding trust.

Transparency isn't just about the present—it's about creating a new, honest dynamic for the future. Over time, as consistency builds, your partner will feel more secure and trusting in the relationship.

---

2. Give Reassurance

Reassurance is another critical element in rebuilding trust. When trust has been damaged, especially after a betrayal, the injured partner may struggle with feelings of doubt, insecurity, or fear of future betrayal. Constant reassurance helps to soothe those fears and reaffirms your commitment to the relationship.

- **Verbal affirmations**: Sometimes, your partner simply needs to hear that you are committed to making the relationship work and that they can trust you again. Use phrases like, "I'm here for you," "I'm committed to fixing this," and "I want to rebuild what we had." These verbal affirmations can help reassure your partner that you're in it for the long haul.

- **Be patient with their insecurities**: After trust has been broken, your partner may have doubts or insecurities that surface more often than before. They may ask for reassurance or question things that wouldn't have been an issue in the past. It's important to approach this with patience and understanding, rather than frustration or defensiveness. Remember, these insecurities are a result of the trust that was broken, and it's your job to help them heal by providing consistent reassurance over time.

- **Show reliability through actions**: Words alone are not enough. Back up your reassurances with consistent actions. Being reliable and dependable goes a long way in demonstrating that you're serious about rebuilding trust. Show up when you say you will, follow through on promises, and make an effort to be emotionally present in the relationship.

- **Understand the need for boundaries**: If your partner requests certain boundaries as part of the healing process (e.g., avoiding specific situations or people), respect those boundaries without hesitation. Their need for boundaries isn't a sign of mistrust—it's a way for them to feel secure as they begin to trust you again. For example, if infidelity was involved, your partner may ask you to limit interactions with certain individuals or be more transparent with your phone usage. While this can feel like a restriction, it's important to view it as a step toward healing rather than a punishment.

Reassurance helps to build emotional security, and over time, consistent reassurance (paired with transparency) can help to alleviate your partner's doubts and fears.

3. Forgive and Seek Forgiveness

Forgiveness is a vital part of rebuilding trust, but it's also one of the most challenging. Genuine forgiveness involves letting go of anger and resentment, which allows both partners to move forward instead of being stuck in the past. However, forgiveness must be sincere—simply saying the words without truly feeling them won't allow for real healing.

- **Seeking forgiveness**: If you've broken your partner's trust, it's essential to seek their forgiveness in a way that shows true remorse. Acknowledge the pain you've caused and take full responsibility for your actions without making excuses. For example, saying, "I'm sorry if I hurt you," minimizes the impact. Instead, say, "I'm deeply sorry for hurting you, and I take full responsibility for what I've done. I understand how this has affected you, and I'm committed to making things right."

- **Give your partner time to forgive**: Forgiveness is a process, and it doesn't happen overnight. Your partner may need time to fully come to terms with what happened and to trust that it won't happen again. It's important to allow them to take that time without rushing or pressuring them to forgive before they're ready. Constantly asking, "Have you forgiven me yet?" can create more pressure and tension, which can hinder healing.

- **Offering forgiveness**: If you are the one who has been hurt, offering forgiveness is equally important for your own healing. Holding onto resentment and anger can poison the relationship over time, preventing true reconciliation. However, don't force yourself to forgive before you're ready. Take the time to work through your emotions and, if necessary, seek professional help to process the pain.

- **Seek professional help if necessary**: When trust has been deeply broken—such as in the case of infidelity or long-term deceit—professional help can be invaluable. A couples therapist can help both partners process their emotions and communicate effectively. Therapy provides a neutral space where both partners can express their feelings, and the therapist can guide you through the forgiveness and healing process in a healthy way.

- **Focus on rebuilding, not punishing**: Once forgiveness is in motion, focus on rebuilding the relationship rather than punishing your partner for their past mistakes. Holding onto grudges or using past mistakes as a weapon in arguments will only prolong the healing process. Forgiveness is about letting go of the past and working together toward a healthier, stronger future.

Forgiveness is a mutual process that allows both partners to heal and move forward. By seeking forgiveness and offering it in return, you create the emotional foundation necessary to rebuild trust.

Conclusion: Rebuilding Trust Takes Time and Commitment

Rebuilding trust is a slow, delicate process that requires full commitment from both partners. Transparency, reassurance, and forgiveness are essential tools for restoring the emotional foundation of the relationship. Through honesty, consistency, and patience, it's possible to rebuild what was broken and emerge with a stronger, more resilient bond.

Remember that trust is rebuilt not just through words, but through consistent actions over time. While the process may be difficult, the rewards of restoring trust can lead to a deeper, more connected relationship that is built on mutual respect and emotional intimacy.

Reevaluate and Make Changes If Necessary

Reevaluating your relationship and making necessary changes is a crucial step in the healing process. As you work on rebuilding trust, addressing communication issues, and fostering emotional intimacy, it's essential to monitor your progress and adjust your approach as needed. This ensures that both partners are on the same page and that any remaining issues are identified and addressed before they escalate further.

---

1. Monitor Progress

Regularly checking in with your partner about how things are going allows both of you to assess the state of the relationship. This ongoing dialogue helps you understand what's working and what needs improvement. It also reinforces that both partners are committed to the process of healing.

- **Schedule regular check-ins**: Designate time to discuss the relationship, focusing on how each partner feels about the progress being made. This could be a weekly or bi-weekly meeting dedicated solely to relationship matters. Creating a safe environment for these discussions is key; ensure that both partners feel comfortable expressing their thoughts without fear of judgment.

- **Ask open-ended questions**: Encourage your partner to share their feelings by asking open-ended questions such as:
    - "How do you feel about the changes we've made so far?"
    - "What areas do you think we still need to work on?"
    - "Are there any specific concerns you'd like to address?"

These questions promote deeper conversations and allow both partners to express their thoughts freely.

- **Recognize improvements**: Acknowledge the positive changes that have occurred, no matter how small. Celebrating progress can foster a sense of accomplishment and motivate both partners to continue working on the relationship. For example, if communication has improved, highlight specific instances where you felt heard and understood.

- **Identify areas needing work**: During these check-ins, be honest about areas that may still require attention. It's crucial to identify ongoing challenges early on. If one partner feels that their emotional needs are still not being met, for instance, this should be addressed promptly. Instead of letting these issues fester, bringing them up allows for constructive discussions and solutions.

- **Keep the tone constructive**: While discussing progress and areas for improvement, it's important to maintain a supportive and constructive tone. Avoid blaming or accusing language, and instead focus on collaboration. Use "we" language to emphasize teamwork. For example, say, "We've made progress, but I think we can work together on improving our communication even more."

Monitoring progress regularly reinforces accountability for both partners and creates an environment of open communication and cooperation, ultimately strengthening the relationship.

---

2. Be Realistic

While it's essential to put in effort to save a relationship, it's equally important to recognize when things are beyond repair. Sometimes, despite the best intentions and hard work, a relationship may be too damaged to salvage. Acknowledging this reality can be difficult but is crucial for both partners' emotional well-being.

- **Assess the relationship honestly**: Reflect on the overall dynamics of the relationship. Are both partners actively engaged in the healing process? Is there a willingness to change and grow? It's important to evaluate whether both partners are equally invested in improving the relationship or if one person is putting in more effort than the other. Unequal investment can lead to resentment and further distance.

- **Look for patterns**: Pay attention to recurring issues or patterns of behavior. If the same problems keep resurfacing despite efforts to address them, it may be a sign that deeper incompatibilities exist. For instance, if communication issues continue to lead to arguments, and both partners struggle to change their patterns, it may indicate a fundamental mismatch in how each person approaches conflict resolution.

- **Identify emotional safety**: Consider whether both partners feel emotionally safe in the relationship. Trust and emotional safety are paramount for a healthy partnership. If either partner feels continually threatened, belittled, or disrespected, it may be time to reconsider the viability of the relationship. Being in an environment where you feel unsafe or unsupported can lead to long-term emotional damage.

- **Recognize when you're not growing**: A

healthy relationship should foster personal growth and mutual support. If you find that the relationship stifles your personal development or makes you feel stuck, it may be worth reassessing. Both partners should feel empowered to pursue their individual goals while being supportive of each other.

- **Consider professional help**:

Sometimes, a neutral third party can provide valuable insights and facilitate discussions that may lead to breakthroughs. A couples therapist can help you evaluate the relationship's viability, guide you through difficult conversations, and offer strategies for improvement. They can also assist in determining whether the relationship is fundamentally salvageable or if it's best for both partners to part ways.

- **Trust your instincts**: If you consistently feel unhappy or unfulfilled despite efforts to improve the relationship, listen to those feelings. Your emotional well-being is paramount, and ignoring red flags can lead to deeper emotional pain down the line.

It's important to approach this step with compassion for both yourself and your partner. Ending a relationship can be one of the most challenging decisions to make, but sometimes it is necessary for both partners to find happiness and fulfillment.

Conclusion: The Importance of Reevaluation

Reevaluating the relationship and making necessary changes is a vital part of the healing process. Monitoring progress through regular check-ins and honest discussions promotes accountability and keeps both partners aligned. However, it's equally crucial to remain realistic about the relationship's potential for recovery.

If you find that the relationship is not progressing, or if both partners are not equally committed to change, it may be time to consider whether it's worth continuing. Trust your instincts and prioritize your emotional health, whether that means working to rebuild the relationship or choosing to move on. Ultimately, the goal should be a healthy, fulfilling partnership—whether that's together or apart.

4 INTIMACY AND PROFESSIONAL HELP

Reignite Intimacy and Passion

Emotional and physical intimacy serve as the glue that holds relationships together. Over time, life stresses, routines, and unresolved conflicts can lead to a decline in affection and passion. If you find that intimacy has faded, it's essential to take proactive steps to rekindle that connection. By prioritizing both emotional and physical closeness, you can create a loving environment where intimacy flourishes.

1. Prioritize Physical Touch

Physical touch is a fundamental expression of love and affection that can significantly enhance intimacy in a relationship. It's important to foster closeness not just in the bedroom, but throughout daily life.

- **Incorporate small gestures**: Simple acts like holding hands, hugging, or gentle touches on the arm can help maintain a sense of closeness and connection. These gestures remind both partners of their affection and strengthen emotional bonds. Consider making a habit of touching each other more throughout the day, even if it's just a brief brush of the hand or a playful nudge.

- **Create a routine for physical connection**: Establish a routine that prioritizes physical touch. This could be as simple as sitting close together while watching TV or taking a moment to embrace when one partner comes home. These small, regular touches can create a foundation for deeper intimacy.

- **Explore touch beyond the bedroom**: Physical touch should extend beyond sexual intimacy. Cuddle on the couch, dance in the living room, or give each other massages. Creating an atmosphere where touch is normalized and celebrated can help both partners feel more comfortable expressing their affection physically.

- **Be mindful of each other's comfort levels**: Understand that everyone has different comfort levels when it comes to physical touch, especially after a period of emotional distance. Pay attention to your partner's reactions and communicate openly about what feels good and what doesn't. Establishing mutual comfort can gradually enhance physical closeness.

---

2. Have Meaningful Dates

Setting aside time for meaningful dates is vital

in rekindling intimacy and passion. Engaging in shared experiences allows couples to reconnect and rediscover the joy of being together.

- **Plan regular date nights**: Dedicate specific evenings for date nights, whether at home or out. This doesn't have to be extravagant; even a simple dinner together can be an opportunity to reconnect. Create a calendar for these dates to ensure they become a priority.

- **Try new activities together**: Engaging in new experiences can reignite excitement and passion in the relationship. Explore hobbies or activities that interest both partners, such as cooking classes, hiking, or art workshops. New experiences can foster deeper conversations and create lasting memories, reinforcing emotional intimacy.

- **Create a romantic atmosphere at home**: If going out is not feasible, transform your home into a romantic setting. Light candles, prepare a nice meal, or even have a picnic indoors. This effort signals to your partner that you value spending quality time together, even in a more casual setting.
- **Focus on fun and joy**: It's important to focus on having fun and enjoying each other's company during these dates. Laughing together, reminiscing about fond memories, and creating new ones can help strengthen your emotional bond and rekindle that

spark of passion.

3. Communicate Sexual Needs

Open and honest communication about sexual needs is crucial for a fulfilling intimate life. Many couples struggle with intimacy issues due to misunderstandings or unexpressed desires.

- **Create a safe space for discussion**: Approach conversations about intimacy with sensitivity and openness. Ensure both partners feel safe to share their thoughts and feelings without judgment. This might involve setting aside time to discuss desires and preferences without distractions.

- **Express your needs and desires**: Be clear about what you want from your intimate life. If there are specific things that you desire or that your partner enjoys, express those openly. Use "I" statements to communicate your feelings, such as "I feel more connected when we spend time together like this" or "I would love to try this in our intimate life."

- **Discuss comfort zones**: It's important to talk about what both partners are comfortable with regarding intimacy. Establishing clear boundaries allows both partners to feel secure in their expressions of love and affection.

- **Gradually rekindle physical passion**: If intimacy has been lacking for some time, it may be helpful to take gradual steps toward rekindling physical passion. Start by focusing on emotional closeness—cuddling, kissing, or holding hands—before transitioning to more intimate activities. This gradual approach can help both partners feel more comfortable and reconnected.

- **Encourage feedback**: Encourage your partner to share their needs and desires, too. This two-way dialogue fosters mutual understanding and respect for each other's feelings, allowing you both to explore your intimate life together.

4. Practice Gratitude

Practicing gratitude is a powerful way to enhance emotional intimacy in a relationship. Acknowledging and appreciating your partner's efforts fosters a positive environment that encourages deeper connections.

- **Express appreciation regularly**: Make it a habit to thank your partner for small acts of kindness. Whether they made dinner, took care of a chore, or simply listened to you after a long day, verbalizing your gratitude reinforces their efforts and shows that you value them.

- **Keep a gratitude journal**: Consider keeping a shared gratitude journal where both partners can write down things they appreciate about each other. This can be a fun and thoughtful exercise that helps reinforce positive feelings and reminds both partners of their love and commitment.

- **Highlight the little things**: It's often the small gestures that mean the most. Comment on the little things your partner does that make your day better. For example, if your partner sends you a sweet text during the day or picks up your favorite snack, acknowledging these actions shows that you notice and appreciate their thoughtfulness.

- **Celebrate milestones and successes**: Celebrate both big and small milestones in your relationship. Whether it's an anniversary, a promotion at work, or simply getting through a tough week, recognizing and celebrating these moments fosters a sense of partnership and mutual support.

- **Create rituals of appreciation**: Consider establishing rituals where you take time each week or month to share what you appreciate about each other. This could be a dedicated time during a date night or a moment before bed. Rituals of appreciation create a consistent space for gratitude, reinforcing emotional intimacy.

Conclusion: Rekindling Intimacy and Passion

Reigniting intimacy and passion requires conscious effort, open communication, and a commitment to nurturing the emotional and physical connection within the relationship. By prioritizing physical touch, setting aside time for meaningful dates, openly discussing sexual needs, and practicing gratitude, couples can create an environment where intimacy flourishes.

Remember that building intimacy takes time, and it's essential to approach the process with patience and understanding. By actively engaging in these practices, you can strengthen the bond between you and your partner, fostering a deeper, more fulfilling relationship filled with love and passion.

Seek Professional Help

When a relationship faces challenges, sometimes the best course of action is to seek professional help. A neutral third party can offer fresh perspectives, facilitate difficult conversations, and provide structured support to help couples navigate their issues. Here are some effective options for seeking professional assistance:

---

1. Consider Couples Therapy
Couples therapy is a valuable resource for partners looking to address their relationship challenges. A trained therapist can help facilitate open communication and provide tools for conflict resolution.

Safe Environment for Expression: Couples therapy creates a controlled, safe space where both partners can express their feelings without fear of judgment or escalation. A therapist helps guide the conversation, ensuring that each partner is heard and understood. This can be particularly beneficial for couples who have struggled to communicate effectively on their own.

Professional Guidance: Therapists are trained to identify underlying issues that may not be immediately obvious to the couple. They can help uncover patterns of behavior, historical grievances, or emotional wounds that are contributing to the current struggles. By addressing these root causes, couples can work towards healing and rebuilding their relationship.

Actionable Solutions: Therapists provide practical strategies tailored to the couple's unique dynamics. They might introduce techniques for better communication, conflict resolution, or emotional regulation. For example, they might suggest specific exercises for active listening or role-playing scenarios to practice handling difficult discussions.

Accountability: Attending therapy sessions can instill a sense of accountability in both partners. The commitment to work on the relationship together can motivate individuals to implement the strategies discussed in sessions. Regular check-ins with a therapist help couples stay focused on their goals and encourage progress.

Emotional Support: Therapy can be an emotional support system for both partners. Discussing relationship issues can bring up intense feelings, and having a professional to guide and support the couple through these emotions can be incredibly helpful. The therapist can also help both partners develop coping mechanisms for stress and anxiety related to the relationship.

---

3. Join Relationship Workshops

In addition to therapy, relationship workshops can

be an excellent way for couples to strengthen their emotional bonds and learn effective communication strategies in a more interactive setting.

Structured Learning Environment: Workshops often offer structured programs designed to teach couples essential skills for maintaining a healthy relationship. Topics may include communication techniques, conflict resolution, emotional intelligence, and intimacy enhancement.

Interactive Exercises: Many workshops incorporate hands-on exercises that encourage couples to practice their newly learned skills in a supportive environment. For example, couples might engage in role-playing scenarios or group discussions that facilitate deeper understanding and connection.

Connection with Other Couples: Participating in workshops provides an opportunity to connect with other couples facing similar challenges. Sharing experiences with peers can help reduce feelings of isolation and foster a sense of community. Hearing different perspectives can also offer valuable insights and strategies that couples might not have considered.

Professional Facilitation: Most workshops are led by experienced facilitators, such as therapists or relationship coaches, who guide couples through the process and offer expertise. These professionals can tailor discussions and activities to the needs of the group, ensuring that everyone benefits from the experience.

Variety of Formats: Workshops can range from a few hours to several days and may be offered in person or online. This flexibility allows couples to choose a format that fits their schedules and comfort levels.

---

4. Work with a Life Coach

If the idea of therapy feels daunting or if couples are looking for a more practical approach to improving their relationship, working with a life coach can be an effective alternative.

Focus on Actionable Strategies: Life coaches often emphasize practical tips and strategies that couples can implement immediately. They help partners identify specific goals for their relationship and develop actionable steps to achieve those goals. For instance, a coach might guide couples in creating a personalized communication plan to address conflicts more effectively.

Personal Development: Life coaches often encourage individuals to focus on their personal growth as well. By working on self-awareness and emotional intelligence, partners can enhance their ability to connect with each other. A coach may suggest exercises for personal reflection or mindfulness practices that foster emotional regulation.

Flexible Approach: Unlike traditional therapy, which may focus on past issues and emotional healing, coaching often has a more forward-looking approach. Coaches help couples focus on future goals and aspirations for their relationship, which can be empowering and motivating.

Convenient Sessions: Coaching sessions can often be more flexible in terms of scheduling and format, accommodating busy lifestyles. Many coaches offer virtual sessions, making it easier for couples to access support regardless of location.

Supportive Accountability: Life coaches can provide ongoing support and accountability, encouraging couples to stay committed to their goals and strategies. Regular check-ins help ensure that both partners remain engaged in the process and continue to make progress.

Conclusion: The Value of Professional Help
Seeking professional help can be a transformative step for couples facing relationship challenges. Whether through couples therapy, relationship workshops, or life coaching, the guidance of a

trained professional can provide valuable insights and strategies for saving the relationship.
By engaging in these processes, couples can enhance their communication, address underlying issues, and strengthen their emotional connection. Professional help offers a structured approach to navigating the complexities of relationships, ultimately leading to a healthier, more fulfilling partnership. Remember, seeking help is a sign of strength and commitment to each other and the relationship.

5 EMOTIONAL AND MENTAL HEALTH

Address Underlying Emotional or Mental Health Issues

Emotional and mental health issues can significantly impact the dynamics of a relationship. They may create barriers to communication, foster misunderstandings, and lead to feelings of isolation between partners. Addressing these underlying issues is crucial for a healthy relationship. Here's a detailed look at how to tackle emotional and mental health challenges effectively.

1. Depression, Anxiety, or Past Trauma

Mental health issues like depression and anxiety can manifest in various ways, affecting not only the individual but also the relationship as a whole.

- **Recognize the signs:** It's essential to be aware of the signs of mental health struggles, which can include withdrawal, irritability, changes in appetite, sleep disturbances, or a lack of interest in activities once enjoyed. If you notice these symptoms in yourself or your partner, it may be time to seek help.

- **Seek Individual Therapy**: Professional therapy can provide a safe space for individuals to explore their feelings and experiences. A qualified therapist can help address the root causes of mental health issues, whether they stem from past trauma, ongoing stressors, or deep-seated emotions. Individual therapy equips individuals with coping strategies and tools to manage their mental health, making them better equipped to contribute positively to the relationship.

- **Open Discussions About Mental Health:** Encourage open conversations about mental health between partners. Discussing feelings of depression or anxiety can help reduce stigma and create a supportive environment. When both partners understand each other's struggles, they can work together to find solutions. For example, if one partner is experiencing anxiety, the other can learn techniques to offer support, such as being patient during anxious moments or creating a calming atmosphere.

- **Consider Joint Therapy**: Sometimes, individual therapy may lead to joint therapy sessions where both partners can explore how mental health issues affect their relationship. This approach can facilitate mutual understanding and help both partners develop strategies for supporting each other.

---

2. Stress Management

Daily stressors can easily seep into a relationship, creating tension and conflict. It's essential to address stress both individually and as a couple.

- **Identify Stressors:** Encourage both partners to identify specific sources of stress, whether they arise from work, family responsibilities, financial pressures, or other obligations. Understanding these stressors can help each partner approach them more effectively.

- **Practice Stress-Relief Techniques:** Engaging in stress-relief techniques can be incredibly beneficial for both partners. Here are some effective methods:

    o **Mindfulness and Meditation:** Practicing mindfulness or meditation can help individuals manage anxiety and stress by fostering a sense of calm and present awareness. Even a few minutes of deep breathing or guided meditation can significantly reduce stress levels.

- o **Physical Activity:** Exercise is a powerful tool for stress relief. Whether it's going for a run, practicing yoga, or taking a dance class together, physical activity releases endorphins, which improve mood and reduce tension.

- o **Hobbies and Interests:** Encourage each other to engage in hobbies or activities that bring joy and relaxation. This could include painting, gardening, reading, or any activity that helps individuals unwind and recharge.

- **Encourage Supportive Practices:** Support each other in developing healthy coping mechanisms. For instance, partners can establish a ritual of sharing their highs and lows at the end of each day, which allows for emotional expression and support.

- **Set Boundaries:** Establishing boundaries regarding work and personal time can also help manage stress. Discuss and agree on limits to work-related activities at home, ensuring that both partners have dedicated time for relaxation and connection.

---

3. Emotional Connection

Emotional disconnection can occur in relationships even in the absence of clear conflict. It's essential to prioritize emotional intimacy to strengthen the bond between partners.

- **Regular Check-Ins:** Make it a habit to regularly check in with each other about feelings and emotional states. Ask open-ended questions like, "How have you been feeling lately?" or "Is there anything on your mind you'd like to share?" This creates an opportunity for dialogue and reinforces that both partners care about each other's emotional well-being.

- **Practice Active Listening:** When discussing feelings, practice active listening by giving full attention and validating your partner's emotions. Show empathy and understanding by responding with phrases like, "That sounds really tough" or "I can see why you'd feel that way." This helps your partner feel heard and valued, which fosters emotional connection.

- **Engage in Shared Activities:** Spend quality

time together engaging in activities that foster connection, such as cooking together, taking walks, or participating in a shared hobby. These experiences create opportunities for deeper conversations and emotional bonding.

- **Express Affection:** Show affection in both small and significant ways. Compliment your partner, express gratitude, or simply hold their hand. Physical affection can help reinforce emotional connections and create a sense of security in the relationship.

- **Be Vulnerable:** Vulnerability can enhance emotional intimacy. Share your own fears, dreams, and aspirations with your partner. Being open about your feelings encourages your partner to reciprocate, creating a deeper emotional bond.

Conclusion: The Importance of Addressing Emotional and Mental Health Issues

Addressing underlying emotional and mental health issues is crucial for a thriving relationship. By recognizing signs of mental health struggles, practicing stress management techniques, and fostering emotional connection, couples can work together to create a supportive and loving environment.

Seeking individual therapy, engaging in stress-relief activities, and maintaining open communication about emotional states can significantly improve the relationship dynamics. Remember, prioritizing mental health and emotional intimacy not only strengthens the partnership but also contributes to personal well-being, creating a healthier, happier relationship for both partners.

6 EMOTIONAL SUPPORT

Strengthen Emotional Support and Partnership
Creating a strong emotional foundation in a relationship is essential for its longevity and fulfillment. When both partners feel supported, appreciated, and encouraged, they can navigate challenges more effectively and cultivate a deeper bond. Here's a detailed look at how to strengthen emotional support and partnership in your relationship.

---

1. Show Appreciation

Expressing gratitude and appreciation is fundamental to maintaining a healthy relationship.

It fosters positive feelings and reinforces the emotional connection between partners.

- **Practice Daily Gratitude**: Make it a habit to express gratitude daily. Simple acknowledgments, such as saying "thank you" for small gestures—like making coffee or taking out the trash—can have a significant impact. These little expressions create a culture of appreciation and remind both partners of the positive contributions they make to each other's lives.

- **Use Specific Praise**: Instead of general statements like "I appreciate you," be specific about what you value. For example, say, "I really appreciate how you listened to me yesterday when I was feeling overwhelmed." Specific praise shows your partner that you notice and value their efforts, making your appreciation feel more genuine and impactful.

- **Celebrate Milestones**: Acknowledge special occasions, such as anniversaries, promotions, or personal achievements. Celebrating these milestones together strengthens your bond and creates shared memories that deepen your connection.

- **Create a Gratitude Ritual**: Establish a routine where both partners take time to share what they appreciate about each other. This could be during a meal, before bedtime, or at the end of the week. Sharing what you value helps both partners feel recognized and strengthens the emotional bond.

- **Written Notes or Messages**: Leave small notes of appreciation in unexpected places, like in your partner's bag or on the bathroom mirror. These surprises serve as tangible reminders of your gratitude and can brighten their day.

---

2. Support Each Other's Growth

Encouraging each other's personal growth is vital for creating a supportive partnership. When partners feel that their aspirations are valued, it strengthens their connection and fosters a sense of teamwork.

- **Encourage Career Aspirations**: If your partner is pursuing career goals, be an active supporter. Ask about their progress, offer to help them prepare for an interview, or celebrate their accomplishments. Being involved in each other's professional lives reinforces the idea that you are a united front, cheering each other on.

- **Explore Hobbies Together**: Engage in each other's hobbies or interests. If your partner enjoys painting, join them for a session or show interest in their work. Shared activities not only strengthen your emotional bond but also provide opportunities for personal growth and enjoyment.

- **Set Personal Goals Together**: Discuss your individual goals and aspirations openly. Whether it's fitness, education, or personal development, talk about how you can support each other in achieving these goals. For instance, you could set a goal to read a certain number of books together or take a class in something new.

- **Create an Environment of Encouragement**: Foster a culture of encouragement by being your partner's cheerleader. Encourage them to pursue new opportunities, even if they seem daunting. Remind them of their strengths and capabilities, helping to boost their confidence.

- **Be Open to Change**: Recognize that growth often involves change, which can sometimes lead to feelings of uncertainty. Approach these changes with an open mind, and be willing to adapt to new dynamics in the relationship as both partners evolve.

---

3. Be Patient with Progress

Improvements in relationships take time, and it's crucial for both partners to be patient with each other throughout this journey.

- **Acknowledge the Process**: Understand that meaningful change doesn't happen overnight. Relationships evolve gradually, and recognizing this can help manage expectations. Celebrate the small steps taken towards improvement rather than focusing solely on the end goal.

- **Set Realistic Goals**: Instead of expecting immediate results, set achievable short-term goals for your relationship. This could include committing to regular date nights, practicing effective communication techniques, or focusing on conflict resolution. Smaller, realistic goals allow both partners to feel accomplished as they work together.

- **Practice Self-Compassion**: Understand that both partners are human and will make mistakes along the way. Practice self-compassion and extend that to your partner. If a particular strategy or effort doesn't yield the desired results, don't be quick to criticize. Instead, view setbacks as opportunities for learning and growth.

- **Celebrate Small Wins**: Take the time to celebrate small victories along the way. If you successfully navigate a difficult conversation or make progress on a shared goal, acknowledge and celebrate these achievements together. This practice reinforces positive behavior and fosters motivation to continue improving.

- **Maintain Open Communication**: Keep the lines of communication open about your progress and feelings. Regularly check in with each other to discuss what's working, what isn't, and how you both feel about the changes. Open communication fosters a sense of teamwork and allows for adjustments along the way.

Conclusion: The Power of Emotional Support and Partnership

Strengthening emotional support and partnership is crucial for a lasting and fulfilling relationship. By showing appreciation, supporting each other's growth, and being patient with the process of improvement, couples can create a strong foundation built on love, trust, and mutual respect.

As partners invest in each other's happiness and success, they nurture a relationship that thrives on teamwork and emotional intimacy. Remember, a supportive partnership is a powerful catalyst for personal growth, relationship satisfaction, and overall happiness. By prioritizing these aspects, you can cultivate a loving environment where both partners feel valued, understood, and connected.

7 WORK ON YOURSELF

Work on Yourself

Personal growth is a powerful and often overlooked element in improving a relationship. When you invest time in yourself, you indirectly improve your emotional health, self-confidence, and ability to contribute positively to the relationship. Here's how focusing on your well-being and self-awareness can enhance both your personal life and your partnership.

---

1. Self-Care: Prioritize Your Physical and Emotional Well-Being

Self-care involves taking deliberate steps to maintain your physical and mental health. It's essential because when you are emotionally and physically balanced, you are better equipped to handle relationship challenges and support your partner.

- **Physical Health**:

    o **Exercise Regularly**: Engaging in regular physical activity boosts endorphins, improves mood, and reduces stress. Physical fitness also contributes to higher self-esteem, which can positively impact how you show up in the relationship.

    o **Eat Well**: A balanced, nutritious diet fuels your body and mind, keeping your energy levels steady. Healthy eating habits can also prevent mood swings, which can lead to unnecessary conflict or miscommunication in relationships.

    o **Sleep**: Adequate sleep is critical for emotional regulation and mental clarity. A well-rested mind is more patient, empathetic, and capable of dealing with stress, which can directly improve relationship interactions.

- **Emotional Self-Care**:

    o **Relaxation and Stress Management**: Incorporating relaxation techniques such as meditation, yoga, or simply taking time for yourself to unwind helps reduce anxiety and keeps you emotionally grounded. Practicing mindfulness, for instance, can help you stay calm in the face of relationship challenges, reducing reactivity in difficult situations.

o **Set Boundaries**: Part of self-care is learning to set boundaries, both in and outside the relationship. This ensures you have time for yourself and can maintain a healthy emotional balance without feeling overwhelmed or losing your individuality.

- **Make Time for Hobbies**: Engaging in activities that you love helps you maintain a sense of self. Whether it's painting, reading, or hiking, nurturing your passions makes you a happier, more fulfilled person, which will have a positive ripple effect in your relationship.

---

2. Develop Emotional Intelligence

Emotional intelligence (EI) refers to the ability to understand, manage, and express your emotions effectively. High emotional intelligence is crucial in relationships because it allows you to handle conflicts calmly, communicate your feelings clearly, and empathize with your partner.

- **Understand Your Emotions**: Start by becoming more aware of your emotional patterns. Ask yourself what situations tend to trigger anger, sadness, or frustration. Recognizing your emotional triggers allows you to pause and think before reacting, reducing the likelihood of miscommunication or heated arguments in your relationship.

- **Manage Your Emotions**: Learning to regulate your emotions is key to maintaining harmony in your relationship. Practice self-soothing techniques like deep breathing or taking a break during intense moments. Emotional regulation helps you respond thoughtfully rather than impulsively, leading to healthier and more constructive conversations.

- **Empathy for Yourself and Others**: Developing empathy involves understanding not only your partner's emotions but also your own. Being kind to yourself, especially when you make mistakes, will help you extend that compassion to your partner. By improving your ability to see things from your partner's perspective, you can navigate conflicts with more understanding and patience.

- **Effective Communication**: Emotional

intelligence helps you express your feelings without blame or anger. Practice using "I" statements (e.g., "I feel hurt when...") to communicate emotions without putting your partner on the defensive. Clear and calm communication fosters deeper connection and reduces misunderstandings.

- **Self-Awareness**: Regularly reflect on your behavior and emotions. Journaling, mindfulness meditation, or talking with a therapist can help you gain insights into your emotional patterns. Self-awareness helps you understand how your emotions affect your relationship and what you can do to improve your responses.

---

3. Be Confident in Your Worth

Confidence in your own value is essential for maintaining a healthy relationship. When you know your worth, you're less likely to lose yourself in trying to "fix" everything or overcompensate for relationship issues. A balanced relationship thrives when both individuals have a strong sense of self-worth and independence.

- **Avoid Co-Dependency**: Confidence in your worth helps you avoid falling into the trap of co-dependency, where one person tries to fix the relationship by over-functioning or taking on too much emotional labor. Recognize that it's not your sole responsibility to "save" the relationship. A healthy partnership is a joint effort.

- **Self-Worth and Boundaries**: Knowing your worth allows you to set healthy boundaries in the relationship. It empowers you to say no when necessary and protects your emotional well-being without feeling guilty. Healthy boundaries prevent resentment from building and ensure mutual respect between partners.

- **Recognize Your Strengths**: Reflect on your personal strengths and what you bring to the relationship. This could be your ability to listen, your problem-solving skills, or your creativity. Acknowledging your strengths enhances your self-esteem and helps you contribute positively to the relationship without seeking validation from your partner.

- **Balance Independence and Togetherness**: Confidence in your worth enables you to maintain a healthy balance between individuality and partnership. It's important to nurture your identity and personal goals alongside your relationship. Pursue your dreams, passions, and interests independently, and encourage your partner to do the same. This mutual respect for each other's autonomy enhances the relationship without compromising personal growth.

Conclusion: Personal Growth as a Pathway to a Stronger Relationship

Focusing on yourself is not a selfish act; in fact, it's one of the best ways to contribute to the health and strength of your relationship. By prioritizing self-care, developing emotional intelligence, and building confidence in your worth, you become a more emotionally balanced and empowered partner.

When both individuals in a relationship take responsibility for their personal growth and well-being, the partnership becomes stronger. This creates a solid foundation where each person can bring their best self to the relationship, fostering mutual respect, deeper emotional connection, and a healthy, supportive environment for love to thrive.

Re-establish Common Goals

One of the most important factors in a successful, lasting relationship is having shared goals and dreams. When partners have a clear sense of what they are working toward together, it helps solidify their bond and creates a sense of purpose in the relationship. Re-establishing common goals can reignite connection, deepen mutual respect, and provide a framework for teamwork. Here's how to effectively realign and collaborate on shared dreams and long-term goals in your relationship.

---

1. Work on Shared Dreams

Reconnecting over shared dreams helps remind both partners of the bigger picture. Whether your goals are about building a home, raising a family, traveling, or career aspirations, working toward them together can strengthen your emotional bond and give your relationship direction.

- **Discuss Your Individual and Shared Goals**: It's important to openly communicate about both individual and shared goals. Sometimes life can pull partners in different directions, leading to a sense of disconnection. Have regular conversations about where you both see yourselves in the future—individually and as a couple. For example, ask questions like, "Where do we want to be in five years?" or "What are the things we want to accomplish together?"

- **Focus on Long-term Planning**: Take time to revisit or create long-term goals together. Whether it's buying a house, starting a family, traveling, or planning for retirement, setting these goals helps create a shared vision. It's also important to periodically review these goals to ensure you're both on the same page and working toward them as a team.

- **Break Down Large Goals**: Large, long-term goals can sometimes feel overwhelming. Break them down into smaller, manageable steps. For instance, if you're planning to buy a home, create a timeline that includes saving for a down payment, researching neighborhoods, and setting a budget. Tackling these smaller milestones together not only brings you closer to your goal but also strengthens your partnership along the way.

- **Celebrate Progress Together**: When you achieve milestones toward your shared dreams, take time to celebrate them. Acknowledge the effort and teamwork that went into reaching the goal. Celebrations can be small, like a dinner to acknowledge reaching a savings target, or larger, like a trip to commemorate achieving a significant life goal. These shared moments reinforce your connection and provide positive reinforcement for working together.

- **Adapt as Life Changes**: As life evolves, so do goals. Be willing to revisit your shared dreams periodically, and adjust them as necessary. New opportunities, changes in career, or family dynamics may require flexibility in your plans. The key is to stay connected through ongoing discussions about what you both want out of life and how to navigate those changes together.

---

2. Compromise: The Art of Flexibility

Compromise is essential in any relationship. It requires both partners to make sacrifices at times, while also ensuring that each person's needs and desires are respected. A healthy relationship is built on the ability to balance individual preferences with shared goals, making compromise a necessary skill.

- **Identify Core Needs**: Start by identifying which goals or values are non-negotiable for each of you. These are the core needs or dreams that are most important to you as individuals. For example, one partner may feel strongly about starting a family, while the other may prioritize career advancement. By understanding each other's core desires, you can work together to find a balance that respects both of your priorities.

- **Open Dialogue on Differences**: It's inevitable that there will be differences in how each partner approaches certain goals. Instead of avoiding these differences, address them head on. For example, if one partner is more focused on financial security while the other values spontaneous adventures, have a conversation about how you can incorporate both elements into your shared goals.

- **Flexibility is Key**: Relationships thrive when both partners are willing to be flexible.

Flexibility means being open to adjusting your expectations and making sacrifices when needed. For example, if one partner is eager to move to a new city for a job opportunity, the other might need to compromise on the timing of the move or negotiate what aspects of their life can be maintained in the new environment. Flexibility fosters a sense of partnership and teamwork.

- **Give and Take**: A successful compromise involves both partners giving and taking. It's not about one person always sacrificing their needs or desires for the other. Make sure there's a balance in how often each partner compromises. This ensures that both individuals feel valued and respected in the relationship. For instance, if you compromise on where to live, your partner might compromise on when to start a family.

- **Collaborative Decision-Making**: When negotiating compromises, use a collaborative approach. Focus on finding win-win solutions that allow both partners to feel heard and respected. This could involve brainstorming alternatives or coming up with creative solutions that address both partners' desires. For example, if one partner wants to travel while the other wants to save money, they could agree to budget-friendly trips that satisfy both the desire for adventure and financial prudence.

- **Respect the Outcome of Compromises**: Once a compromise has been reached, it's important to respect the decision and not revisit it with resentment. Trust that both of you made the best decision together, and honor the agreement. This demonstrates that you value your partner's input and are committed to the health of the relationship.

The Importance of Shared Goals and Compromise

Shared goals and the willingness to compromise are crucial for maintaining a strong, healthy relationship. They give both partners a sense of direction and purpose while reinforcing their emotional connection. Working together toward common objectives fosters teamwork and mutual respect, while compromise ensures that both partners' needs are met and that the relationship remains balanced and fulfilling.

When partners are aligned in their goals, they create a shared vision of the future that strengthens their bond. However, flexibility and compromise are equally important. Relationships require adaptability, especially as life circumstances change. By maintaining open communication, identifying core values, and practicing compromise, you can keep your relationship resilient and harmonious.

Through re-establishing common goals and practicing healthy compromise, you and your partner can cultivate a deeper connection and find fulfillment in your shared journey.

9 MANAGE CONFLICT

Manage Conflict Constructively

Conflict is a natural part of any relationship, but how you and your partner handle it determines whether it leads to growth or division. Learning to manage conflict constructively can transform disagreements into opportunities for deeper understanding and connection. Here's how to approach conflict in a way that strengthens your relationship:

1. Avoid Blaming or Name-Calling
2.

When emotions run high during an argument, it can be easy to resort to blaming or name-calling. However, this approach is damaging and

often escalates the conflict, making resolution more difficult. To avoid this, focus on addressing the issue at hand rather than attacking your partner personally.

- **Focus on the Problem, Not the Person**: Instead of saying, "You always do this," reframe your statements to focus on the specific issue. For example, say, "I feel frustrated when this happens because..." This shifts the conversation away from personal attacks and toward problem-solving.

- **Avoid Criticizing Your Partner's Character**: When you criticize your partner's character ("You're so selfish," "You're lazy"), it creates defensiveness and shuts down communication. Instead, address their behavior without making it about who they are as a person. For example, say, "When you don't help with the chores, I feel overwhelmed" rather than "You're never helpful."

- **Be Mindful of Tone and Language**: Your tone can make a huge difference in how your words are received. Using a calm, respectful tone encourages more productive conversations. Harsh or sarcastic tones, on the other hand, can lead to feelings of hurt and resentment, making conflict resolution more difficult.

---

3. Practice Fair Fighting

Fair fighting means arguing in a way that is respectful, focused, and constructive. It's about keeping the discussion on track, maintaining emotional control, and working toward a resolution rather than rehashing old wounds.

- **Focus on One Issue at a Time**: Bringing up multiple grievances during an argument can overwhelm your partner and prevent resolution. Stick to the current issue without dredging up past mistakes. This helps keep the conversation focused and productive, rather than spiraling into a cycle of blame. For instance, if you're upset about how money is being managed, stick to that topic without veering off into unrelated issues like household chores or past disagreements.

- **Don't Bring Up Past Mistakes**: When we're hurt, it's tempting to bring up past wrongs during a new argument. However, this prevents healing and resolution. Focus on resolving the current conflict instead of reliving old ones. If past issues need to be addressed, do so separately at a time when emotions are calmer.

- **Take Breaks If Needed**: If you or your partner start to feel overwhelmed or too emotional during a conflict, it's okay to take a break. Stepping away allows both of you to cool down and gather your thoughts before continuing the discussion. Agree on a time to revisit the conversation, and use the break to reflect rather than to avoid the issue.

- **Stay Calm and Composed**: Emotional outbursts often escalate conflict rather than solve it. Practice calming techniques such as deep breathing or counting to ten to manage your emotions during a heated argument. Remaining calm helps keep the conversation respectful and solution-focused.

---

4. Look for Win-Win Solutions

In relationships, it's important to approach conflict with the mindset that you and your partner are on the same team. Instead of trying to "win" the argument or prove that you are right, work together to find a solution that benefits both of you. This cooperative approach fosters mutual respect and a stronger bond.

- **Avoid the Need to "Win" the Argument**: In a relationship, winning an argument should not be the goal. If one partner "wins," it often means the other feels unheard or defeated, which can lead to resentment. Instead, aim to reach a compromise where both partners feel their needs have been acknowledged and respected.

- **Collaborate on Solutions**: Frame the conflict as a problem that you both need to solve together. This shifts the focus from opposition to collaboration. For example, if you're arguing about how to spend free time, brainstorm ways to balance both of your desires rather than

- insisting on one solution. Ask each other, "How can we make this work for both of us?"

- **Compromise**: Relationships thrive on compromise, where both partners are willing to give a little to achieve a solution. Compromise does not mean sacrificing your needs entirely, but rather finding a middle ground that you can both agree on. Be willing to listen to your partner's perspective and see where you can be flexible. For example, if you're deciding how to divide household chores, each partner might take on tasks they're less enthusiastic about, knowing it contributes to the relationship's overall harmony.

- **Seek Mutual Understanding**: Try to understand where your partner is coming from. This involves active listening and empathy. Even if you disagree, acknowledging your partner's feelings can help defuse the situation and lead to a more constructive dialogue. Phrases like "I can see why you feel that way" or "I understand your perspective" can go a long way in calming tensions.

---

5. Create a Plan for Future Conflicts

Conflict in relationships is inevitable, but it doesn't have to be destructive. By creating a strategy for handling future disagreements, you can avoid escalation and promote healthy communication.

- **Agree on Ground Rules**: Establish rules for how you will handle conflicts in the future. These could include avoiding name-calling, taking breaks if needed, or focusing on one issue at a time. Having these guidelines in place helps both partners feel more secure during heated moments.

- **Check-in Regularly**: Have regular relationship check-ins where you discuss how things are going, outside of conflict situations. This proactive approach helps address small issues before they become major conflicts. It also ensures that both partners feel heard and valued.

- **Repair After Conflict**: After an argument, it's important to repair any emotional damage that might have occurred. This can involve apologizing if necessary, offering reassurance, or simply spending quality time together to reconnect. Repairing after conflict strengthens the bond and prevents lingering resentment.

Conclusion: Turning Conflict into Growth
Managing conflict constructively is a key component of a healthy, thriving relationship. It's not about avoiding conflict altogether but about handling disagreements in a way that promotes understanding, respect, and mutual growth.
By avoiding blame, practicing fair fighting, and working toward win-win solutions, you can turn

conflicts into opportunities to deepen your connection and strengthen your relationship. With a focus on collaboration rather than competition, both partners can feel heard, respected, and supported, leading to a more harmonious and fulfilling partnership.

10 BOUNDARIES

Set Boundaries and Expectations

Establishing clear boundaries and expectations is a crucial aspect of maintaining a healthy and balanced relationship. Boundaries protect emotional and personal well-being while ensuring mutual respect, trust, and understanding between partners. Setting these limits helps prevent misunderstandings and fosters a relationship where both individuals feel secure, valued, and respected. Below are detailed insights on how to set and respect boundaries and expectations effectively.

---

1. Establish Healthy Boundaries

Healthy boundaries are the invisible lines that define how you and your partner expect to be treated. These limits are important for maintaining emotional balance, respect, and individual well-being within the relationship. Without clear boundaries, it's easy for misunderstandings, resentment, and over-dependence to occur.

- **Communicate Your Needs**: Boundaries begin with understanding and communicating your own emotional, physical, and personal needs. Be clear with your partner about what makes you feel comfortable or uncomfortable. For example, if you need time alone after a long day to recharge, let your partner know. Similarly, communicate any emotional boundaries, such as how much you're comfortable sharing about sensitive topics or past experiences.

- **Mutual Agreement on Boundaries**: Boundaries should be mutually agreed upon and respected by both partners. Have open conversations where each of you can express your expectations, desires, and limits. For cxample, you may want to discuss how much time you need for yourself, what behaviors are off-limits (such as raising your voice or discussing private matters in public), or how much personal information you're comfortable sharing with friends and family. This collaborative approach ensures that both partners feel secure and respected.

- **Respecting Boundaries**: Once boundaries are set, respecting them is key to maintaining trust and emotional safety. If your partner expresses a boundary, be mindful and avoid crossing it. For example, if your partner has set a boundary around personal space or needing alone time, honor that request without taking it personally. Respecting boundaries builds trust and shows that you value your partner's needs.

- **Revisit and Adjust Boundaries as Needed**: Boundaries are not set in stone. As individuals and as a couple, your needs and circumstances may change over time. It's important to periodically check in with each other to see if any boundaries need to be adjusted. This could be especially relevant during major life changes like moving, starting a family, or career shifts. Regularly updating boundaries ensures that both partners continue to feel comfortable and supported.

2. Discuss Expectations Clearly

Having clear expectations about what you both need from the relationship is just as important as setting boundaries. Expectations can range from how much time you spend together to how you communicate during conflicts. Defining and discussing these expectations helps prevent disappointment and misunderstandings.

- **Discuss Expectations for Time Together**: One common area where expectations often differ is in how much time partners expect to spend together. For example, one partner may expect daily quality time, while the other may need more personal space or time with friends. Having an open discussion about how much time you both need for

- connection versus time spent apart ensures that neither partner feels neglected or suffocated. Compromises may be necessary, but it's essential to find a balance that satisfies both.

- **Emotional Support Expectations**: Partners often have different expectations about the level of emotional support they require. Discuss how you prefer to receive emotional support—whether it's through verbal encouragement, physical affection, or simply having someone listen without offering solutions. This clarity can help both partners meet each other's emotional needs effectively and avoid misunderstandings during challenging times.

- **Address Financial Expectations**: Money is one of the most common sources of conflict in relationships. It's important to set expectations around financial matters, such as how much each partner contributes to expenses, savings goals, and spending habits.

If one partner prefers saving for the future while the other enjoys spontaneous spending, having a clear conversation can help align your financial priorities and prevent future conflicts.

- **Expectations Around Conflict Resolution**: How you handle conflict is another area where expectations should be set. Some partners may prefer to resolve issues immediately, while others may need time to cool down before discussing a problem. Discuss how you both prefer to handle disagreements and establish ground rules for fighting fair, such as no name-calling or bringing up past grievances.

3. Respect Each Other's Independence

Healthy relationships require both togetherness and individuality. While it's important to share your life with your partner, it's equally important to maintain your own identity, interests, and personal space. Respecting each other's independence fosters a sense of balance and prevents feelings of

suffocation or dependence in the relationship.

- **Encourage Personal Growth**: Both partners should feel empowered to pursue their own interests, goals, and hobbies outside of the relationship. For instance, if your partner loves art or playing sports, support their participation in those activities even if they don't involve you. Personal growth is essential for long-term happiness, and partners who encourage each other's growth often enjoy a more balanced and fulfilling relationship.

- **Give Each Other Space**: Allowing space for individual time is crucial for maintaining a sense of independence and preventing emotional burnout. This could mean giving your partner time to spend with friends, pursue a hobby, or simply relax alone. For example, some individuals need downtime to recharge after a long day, and respecting that need for space can prevent feelings of being overwhelmed or stifled in the relationship.
- **Avoid Over-dependence**: While emotional support is vital, it's important to maintain a sense of independence rather than relying entirely on your partner for your happiness or well-being. Over-dependence can create pressure in a relationship and may cause one partner to feel overwhelmed or burdened. Cultivating your own social circle, hobbies, and self-care routines helps you maintain a strong sense of self.

- **Balance Togetherness and Autonomy**: Find a balance between spending quality time together and nurturing your individual lives. For example, while you may enjoy weekly date nights or shared activities, also make time for individual hobbies, personal development, and socializing with friends outside of the relationship. This balance strengthens your connection as a couple while allowing each person to grow as an individual.

---

4. Set Boundaries Around External Influences

Sometimes, external factors such as friends, family, or work can influence a relationship in unhealthy ways. It's important to set boundaries regarding how much external influence is allowed into your personal life.

- **Limit Outside Interference**: Family and friends can sometimes overstep boundaries or provide unsolicited advice, which can create tension between partners. It's important to agree on what personal matters you're comfortable sharing with others and which should remain private. For example, if a conflict arises, decide together whether it's appropriate to discuss it with friends or family, or if it's better to keep it between the two of you.

- **Work-Life Boundaries**: Balancing work and personal life is essential. If one partner's job demands excessive time or energy, it's crucial to set boundaries around work hours, especially in terms of how much work spills over into personal time. Agree on limits such as no work emails during dinner or designated times for uninterrupted connection.

Conclusion: Boundaries and Expectations Strengthen Relationships

Setting and maintaining healthy boundaries and expectations is key to building a strong, resilient relationship. Clear communication about what each partner needs, both individually and within the relationship, helps create a sense of security and respect. Boundaries foster emotional safety, while clearly defined expectations prevent misunderstandings and disappointments.

By respecting each other's independence, encouraging personal growth, and maintaining a healthy balance between individuality and togetherness, you can cultivate a relationship where both partners thrive, both as individuals and as a couple. Through mutual respect, open dialogue, and ongoing adjustments as your relationship evolves, boundaries and expectations will continue to strengthen your bond, providing the foundation for long-term happiness and fulfillment.

ABOUT THE AUTHOR

Evelyn started her professional life with a degree from Stanford University. She has taught in several universities and teaching hospitals. She now has her own practice where she takes care of people with many varied emotional issues. She lives alone following the death of her husband, with two large dogs (Rufus and Remus) in a rural community. If she ever has spare time she paints watercolors, and plans to exhibit one day.

www.ingramcontent.com/pod-product-compliance
Lightning Source LLC
Chambersburg PA
CBHW050320230526
45471CB00005B/2276